Crocodiles and Alligators

Experts on child reading levels
have consulted on the level of text and
concepts in this book.

At the end of the book is a "Look Back and Find" section
which provides additional information and encourages
the child to refer back to previous pages
for the answers to the questions posed.

Angela Grunsell trained as a teacher in 1969.
She has a Diploma in Reading and Related Skills
and for the last five years has advised London
teachers on materials and resources.

Published in the United States in 1985 by
Franklin Watts, 387 Park Avenue South, New York, NY10016

© Aladdin Books Ltd/Franklin Watts

Designed and produced by
Aladdin Books Ltd, 70 Old Compton Street, London W1

ISBN 0-531-10099-5

Printed in Belgium

FRANKLIN · WATTS · FIRST · LIBRARY

Crocodiles and Alligators

by
Kate Petty

Consultant
Angela Grunsell

Illustrated by
Karen Johnson

Franklin Watts
New York · London · Toronto · Sydney

Have you ever seen a real prehistoric monster?
There were crocodiles like this living at the
same time as the dinosaurs.
They haven't changed for millions of years.

Crocodiles and alligators belong to the group
of reptiles called crocodilians. They are
the biggest and most intelligent reptiles.
This Nile Crocodile is over five yards long.

Most crocodiles live in tropical places.
Sometimes they dig a hole in the bank.
They can lie absolutely still for hours.
You might mistake one for a floating log.

If an animal comes down alone to the water to drink, the crocodile will move in very fast to catch it. Humans have to take great care near these waters.

Reptiles are cold-blooded animals. They grow as hot or cold as their surroundings. Crocodiles like to bask in the sun. They often yawn like this one. The air on its tongue helps it to cool down.

Like all crocodilians this alligator lives on land and in water. Its webbed feet and strong tail help it to swim fast. It closes up its ears and its throat when it goes underwater.

The American Alligator seems to smile but its teeth are sharp and dangerous. You can only see the upper teeth when its mouth is shut. Its head is squarer than a crocodile's.

You can tell this is a crocodile because some of its lower teeth are showing too. This is a Nile Crocodile.

Young crocodiles feed on fish, frogs and turtles.
Big ones snap at the legs of larger animals,
like antelopes, and drag them under water.
The water softens the meat.

The crocodile tears its food and gulps it without chewing. Sometimes it swallows stones to help grind the food in its stomach.
These crocodiles are sharing their meal.

Like all reptiles, crocodiles lay eggs.
The mother digs out a nest one night and
lays about forty eggs in it. She covers them over
with soil and stays by them until they hatch.

About three months later the baby crocodiles
start to squawk from inside their shells.
When the mother hears them she uncovers the
nest with her claws and helps them to come out.

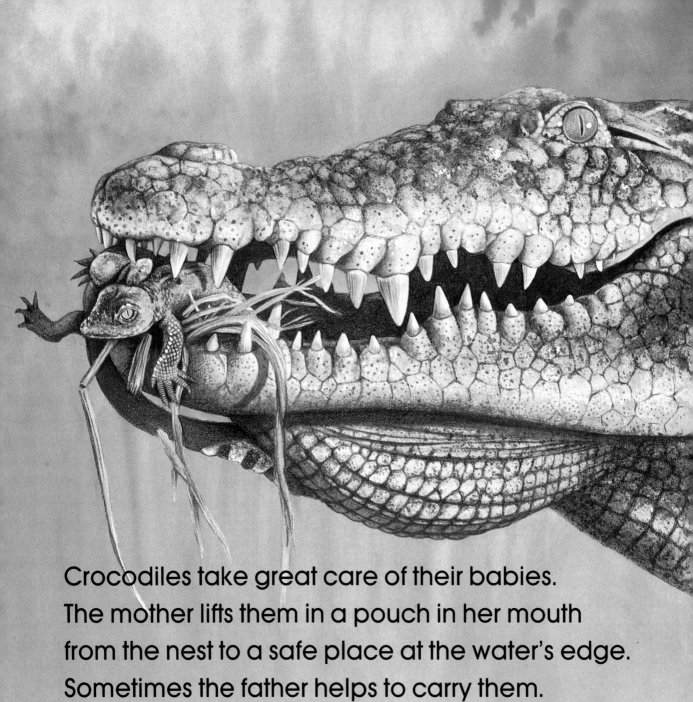

Crocodiles take great care of their babies.
The mother lifts them in a pouch in her mouth
from the nest to a safe place at the water's edge.
Sometimes the father helps to carry them.

18

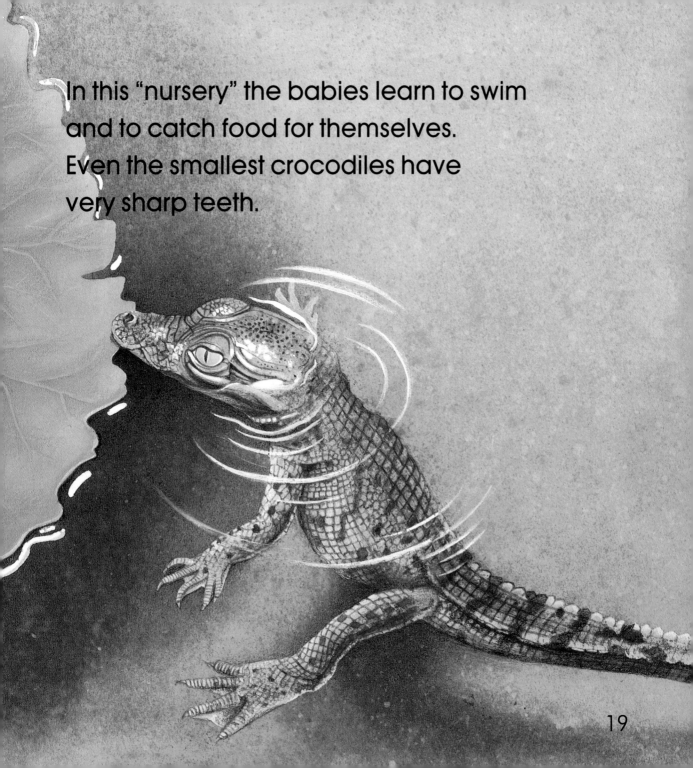

In this "nursery" the babies learn to swim
and to catch food for themselves.
Even the smallest crocodiles have
very sharp teeth.

Baby crocodiles are in great danger from hungry animals, including other crocodiles. A bird like the Goliath Heron can easily pick one up in its long beak.

A crocodile can be frightened by a hippo but its only real enemies are human beings. People hunt them for food and for their skins, which are made into shoes and purses.

These are Saltwater Crocodiles in Australia,
the biggest and most dangerous of them all.
They are known to kill people.
Some can grow up to eleven yards long.

There are twelve sorts of crocodiles but Saltwater Crocodiles are the only ones to swim in the open sea. They don't like rough waves and come inland to find calmer water.

There are two other members of the crocodilian family beside the crocodiles and alligators. This one is the Ghavial, found only in India. They catch fish with their long, thin jaws.

Caimans are found in South America. They are very like alligators except that they have overlapping bony scales on their bellies. This is the Common Caiman.

Soon there might not be many crocodiles left.
This Nile Crocodile is going to a crocodile
preserve where it will be safe from hunters.
Scientists of the preserve study the crocodiles.

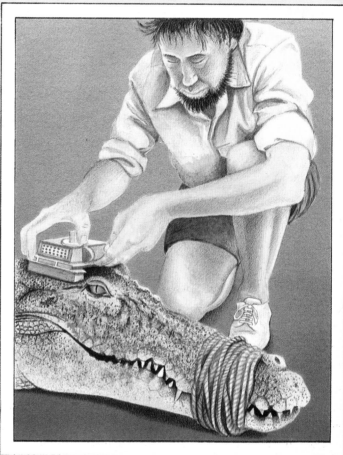

The transmitter on the Saltwater Crocodile's
head will tell the scientists where it is swimming.
They want to protect the crocodiles but
they need to protect themselves first!

27

Look back and find

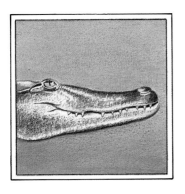

Is this a crocodile or an alligator?

What family of reptiles do crocodiles and alligators belong to?

Do you know some differences between crocodiles and alligators?

What do crocodiles eat?

What happens when two or more crocodiles want to share the kill?
Crocodiles are intelligent. Each one has a place in the group. The most important crocodile will eat first and the others will follow in order of importance.

How many eggs does a mother crocodile lay?

Where do alligators lay their eggs?
Some alligators make nests from rotting leaves. The leaves are warm and help the eggs to hatch.

Where does the mother take the baby crocodiles?

When does a crocodile reach its full size?
Crocodiles never completely stop growing. The largest ones might be 100 years old.

Which is the biggest crocodile of all?

What makes these crocodiles different from other crocodiles?

What is another name for them?
Estuarine Crocodiles, because they prefer estuaries to the open sea.

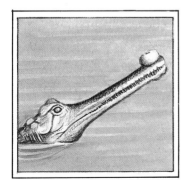

What is this animal called?

Where does it live?

What is the lump on the end of its nose?
It might be a sort of sound box to make its mating call louder.

Index